WARNING

STRESS MAY BE

HAZARDOUS TO YOUR HEALTH

THE STRESS & BURNOUT

AWARENESS & PREVENTION GUIDE

STOP Stress From Manifesting Into Anxiety, Panic Attacks & Agoraphobia

Written by Suzanne J. Price

Author, Coach & Motivational Speaker

www.theoneminutestressmanager.com

The Stress & Burnout

Awareness & Prevention Guide

STOP! Stress From Manifesting Into Anxiety, Panic Attacks & Agoraphobia

Canadian Intellectual Property Certificate of Registration 2012

Published by Suzanne J. Price

ISBN 978-0-9812862-2-8

The Bad News Is....

Stress Is Related To The Six Leading Causes Of Death

It Can and Does Manifest Into

Anxiety, Burnout, Panic Attacks and Agoraphobia

Stress Can Affect Absolutely Anyone &

It Often Seems To Strike Out Of The Blue

The Good News Is...

This Can Be Prevented & It Can Also Be Overcome

Learning How To Recognize The Symptoms And Manage The Stress In Your Life May Be One Of The Most Important Lessons You Could Ever Learn

www.theoneminutestressmanager.com

A Word From The Author

I wrote both, **The Stress & Burnout Awareness & Prevention Guide,** and the follow up book called, **Relieve Stress, Anxiety, Burnout, Panic Attacks & Agoraphobia The Same Way I Did,** in part to launch **The Stress And Burnout Awareness And Prevention Campaign.** Much of what you will find in this book I wrote during the years that I was personally suffering with debilitating stress, anxiety, panic attacks, burnout and agoraphobia, and was desperately looking for a way to overcome it. And throughout the years that followed when I started offering presentations and workshops to teach other's how to manage their stress, and how to use the tools that I used to overcome these debilitating disorders.

That was all a number of years ago and was something that I thought I'd put behind me. But the truth is that since I learnt so much and feel that I do have some advice to share, I feel a sense of responsibility to help others by teaching them the truth about stress.

The reason that I have decided to launch this campaign and release this book now, is because stress and its related disorders are issues that really bother me. Not in the way that I suffer with them anymore, because I now deal with stress better than I have ever done so in the past. But, when talking about these issues, the one thing that really infuriates me is the fact that there really isn't enough being said or done to promote awareness and prevention.

The statistics of stress are staggering. And we in North America are now living in a time and place where we have the highest rates of stress, anxiety and depression in the world. This is nothing new. I know this because I have been watching the statistics about stress for many years. Yet even though we know all this, and we are very aware of how detrimental stress can be to every aspect of a person's life, not to mention their health, there is still nowhere near enough emphasis put on teaching people about the warning signs, and how to prevent their stress from spiraling out of control.

Stress and its related disorders (often labelled as mental illnesses) are usually talked about and treated as though they are *completely* out of our control. And because of this I would guess that there are a lot of people who live under the illusion that these sort of disorders only happen to other people. But this couldn't be any further from the truth.

In fact, the reality is that stress can and does manifest into burnout, anxiety, panic attacks and agoraphobia. It can be debilitating and it often seems to strike out of the blue. It can literally take over every aspect of a person's life, and it can happen to *absolutely* anyone. And that means that it could even happen to you. But most people do not know this, and because they are not aware of the looming dangers, the chances are that they wouldn't be prepared if, or when stress started to creep up on them. And that is when people get taken off guard. This is exactly why I believe that awareness and prevention is such an important issue.

Knowing what I know now, I truly believe that with the right awareness many of these stress related disorders *can* be prevented, and that is exactly why I wrote this book.

My intention with this book, and with the Stress And Burnout Awareness And Prevention Campaign is to bring this much needed information to the forefront. Everyone should know how to recognize the symptoms and warning signs of stress, and know when to take action and jump into prevention mode. We are living in stressful times and in a stressful world, so we absolutely must take this issue seriously. And the one thing we can all do to be proactive is to pay attention to what I have written in this book.

At first glance it may seem ridiculous to think that someone wouldn't recognize when they are suffering with stress, but for reasons which I also explain in this book, it is actually very easy to miss the *real* warning signs, or to recognize what is really *causing* you stress.

With that said, I want to point out that this book is not one that teaches you how to overcome these debilitating disorders, but its purpose is meant more to help you prevent them. And in the process I want to encourage anyone who is already suffering with these debilitating disorders to remain hopeful while knowing that with the right tools, many of these disorders can also be overcome.

In this book I share my story of how I personally suffered with stress which quickly manifested into anxiety, panic attacks, burnout and agoraphobia. And how I failed to recognize that the physical symptoms I was experiencing were in fact symptoms of stress, and looking back were warning signs that I missed. I also share how the doctors who I went to for help failed to put me at ease by not explaining anything to me about what I was suffering with, why this had happened to me or what to expect. And how my lack of understanding about my situation caused more worry and fear that exacerbated the problem. The result being that within a few weeks of my first real warning signs my stress spiraled out of control and manifested into a 10 year struggle with anxiety, panic attacks, burnout and agoraphobia. And this was something that I had never suffered with before.

I also explain how to recognize the symptoms of all of these disorders, and what stress could have in store for you if you chose to ignore the warning signs. And finally I explain why we often fail to recognize that we are suffering the effects of stress, and how easy it can be to get so caught up in the symptoms and the problems which have resulted from the stress, that we fail to see what is really causing the stress in the first place. And finally I also talk about a few of the life skills that can cause stress, and I touch on how lifestyle can also impact the way you experience life. I truly believe that for some, this book could be a lifesaver.

Upon reading this information I'm sure that it will all make sense, and you will be better prepared and more in tune with what is going on in your own life as far as stress is concerned. You may even start to be able recognize stress in someone else, and I can guarantee you will have a better understanding of what it is like for a person who suffers with these disorders.

My goal with this book is to help people become more aware of what stress is, how it can manifest into more debilitating disorders, how to recognize the symptoms and warning signs, and how to recognize what in your life might be causing you stress. It is also my goal to encourage hope in those who suffer with it, by showing that with the right awareness and the right tools it is also possible to overcome this.

Suzanne Price is an author, coach and motivational speaker who lives in Vancouver and who is on a mission to spread awareness about stress and how to prevent it from manifesting into anything more than just that. Stress!

Her efforts are spreading globally through her writing, speaking engagements, webinars, online video and workshops, social media, expert interviews and an online gathering with experts. Suzanne's Kindle books are available around the world and can be translated via Kindle into many languages.

To find out what else Suzanne is up to visit www.suzanneprice.com

Other Books & Programs Written By Suzanne J. Price

Relieve Stress, Anxiety, Burnout, Panic Attacks & Agoraphobia The Same Way I Did

It's Your Life – So What Are You Going To Do With It?

New Year Resolutions, Goals, Dreams & Aspirations

How To Turn That First Glance Into A Date.

Tapping Into Your Mind Body Connection

Table Of Contents

You Are Invited

To A Free

Stress & Burnout Awareness & Prevention

Webinar Hosted By Me – Suzanne Price

Please register on this website
www.theoneminutestressmanager.com

Also while on the site please add your name to my VIP Launch List, and you can gain immediate access to an audio of me talking about my experience with stress, anxiety, burnout, panic attacks and agoraphobia, and listen to how I finally overcame this debilitating disorder after struggling with it for ten years.

The VIP Launch List will allow you to become one of the first to learn about all of my upcoming projects, including:

Book launches – including spontaneous free download days

Webinars

Workshops

Online Programs

Events

Special Offers

Video Launches

Television & Radio Appearances

And much, much more...

You can also join me on Facebook at http://www.facebook.com/TheStressAnxietyBurnoutAwarenessPreventionCampaign or follow me on Twitter at PeoplePoweredCo

I hope this book will serve as a helpful resource and that the information inside will arm you with preventative measures. Don't let stress take control of your life.

I would love some feedback and would really appreciate a review on Amazon if you would be so kind.

Thank you very much for your support, and remember to please join the VIP Launch List at www.theoneminutestressmanager.com

Suzanne

Disclaimer

While reading this book please keep in mind that I am not a trained medical professional nor do I claim to be one. I am in no way suggesting that you use the materials in this book as a substitute for professional help.

I am however someone who has suffered with stress which manifested into burnout, anxiety, panic attacks and agoraphobia which affected every aspect of my life for ten years. However upon finding the right therapies and applying them to the different aspects of my life I fully recovered from these debilitating disorders.

My intentions with this book is to provide you with some general information and guidance as to how to recognize the symptoms, and how to make some lifestyle changes that could help you prevent stress from ever becoming anything more than just that. Stress!

The Grim Statistics Of Stress

It is 2012 and we in North America have the highest rates of stress, anxiety and depression in the world. Drug and alcohol abuse is running rampant, and prescription drug abuse is on the rise.

Stress has also been linked to the 6 leading causes of death, and it is costing North American businesses billions of dollars every year.

Some reports show that 75% of all doctors visits are stress related, at least half of all suspected heart attacks turn out to be a panic attack, and 1 in every 5 people are taking some sort of anti anxiety or anti depressant medication.

Recent studies show that over 80% of university students are so overwhelmed that they feel anxious most of the time, and at least 4 out of 5 people will end up suffering with either some sort of stress or anxiety related disorder, or some type of social phobia throughout their lives. And these statistics do not even take into consideration the amount of people whose lives are affected by daily worries, fears, and phobias.

But wait, it gets worse.

Stress can and does manifest into anxiety, burnout, panic attacks and agoraphobia, and this could happen to YOU!

Learning how to recognize the symptoms of stress, and how to manage the stress in your life could be some of the most important lessons you and your loved ones could ever learn.

Take A Peek At What Stress Could Have In Store For You!

If you have never suffered with anxiety or had the misfortune of having a panic attack then I can guarantee you this. You couldn't even begin to imagine how scary or uncomfortable this can be.

In fact most people who suffer with panic attacks often sum up their experience as feeling as though they are going to faint, that they are having a heart attack, or that they are going to die.

In a nutshell, a panic attack often feels as though all of your senses go haywire, your mind goes into overload, and you experience symptoms and sensations throughout your body that you couldn't possibly replicate no matter how hard you tried.

If you are lucky, when having an attack you will automatically switch into autopilot. This is a godsend that may save you from attracting any unwanted attention to yourself that would only cause embarrassment and add to your stress.

Then when it is all over, if you are fortunate enough to find yourself still standing, you will be left feeling disappointed, disheartened, depleted and even doomed. You'll probably feel disappointed because you just experienced another panic attack, disheartened by the potential of never overcoming them, depleted of your energy because the attack just took so much out of you, and doomed by the prospects that these attacks could potentially control every aspect of your life.

Afterwards, as you try to figure out why you just experienced another devastating attack on your body, you frantically pray that you will never have to go through another one again. And while you desperately search for some sort of permanent solution, you are constantly reminded that the next attack could be looming just around the corner.

Oh and if you are wondering how *I* know this. Well that would be because I suffered with this debilitating condition for well over ten years, and I can assure you, it is a terrifying experience.

However, if there was any good that came out of my own experience of suffering with anxiety, panic attacks and agoraphobia, it would be that I can now help people like you. And because I know firsthand what stress can do to a person, I believe that it would be in everyone's best interest to learn how to recognize the symptoms and the warning signs, to become more aware of what causes stress in your own life, and to learn how to manage your stress.

By arming yourself with the right information you have a much greater chance of preventing something like this from ever happening to you.

Awareness is the key to prevention, and an ounce of prevention is worth a pound of a cure.

With the right awareness these debilitating conditions can be prevented, and with the right tools, they can also be overcome, and that is exactly why I wrote The Stress & Burnout Awareness & Prevention Guide, and Tapping Into Your Mind Body Magic. Both programs are available in print as well as in live, and online workshops.

Stress Can Affect Absolutely Anyone At Anytime And It Often Seems To Strike Out Of The Blue. Learning How To Recognize The Symptoms Could Be One Of The Most Important Lessons You Could Ever Learn

Join me for The Stress & Burnout Awareness And Prevention Webinar to learn more. Register at www.theoneminutestressmanager.com

My Story

It's been 10 years now since I suffered with anxiety, panic attacks and agoraphobia, a debilitating condition that I lived with for *well over* a decade. And although I hope to never have to go through that again, I have to admit that it helped me to discover my true passion and purpose in life.

TO HEAR MY STORY OF HOW

I PERSONALLY OVERCAME

ANXIETY, PANIC ATTACKS AND AGORAPHOBIA

VISIT
http://www.theoneminutestressmanager.com

Or email me at
Suzanne@suzanneprice.com

How It All Started

I have to admit that I had experienced the occasional panic attack before. Once, after an event which left me in fear for my personal safety, and another when I became involved in a business that drained the life out of me, and turned out to be a money pit.

However, this time was different, firstly because there *appeared* to be no apparent reason for the sudden onset of worry and overwhelm. And secondly, the way this all started seemed to have a very different set of symptoms from what I had experienced before.

This time around the first signs of trouble appeared while I was at work when I noticed that I was starting to experience dizzy spells. At first I wondered if I was allergic to something in that environment as I didn't seem to be having this problem anywhere else.

However, in saying that, I had also been having a lot of trouble not sleeping, and had been suffering with chronic tension in my shoulders, neck and back. In fact this tension had gotten so bad that my left side had all but seized up causing me to feel as though I was only breathing through one lung. But like so many people who find themselves under a lot of stress, I had failed to recognize where my physical symptoms had come from. And I certainly was not aware of the connection between any of these things that were going on in my life.

It was only a matter of days before the dizziness and tension had gotten worse and I had started to experience feelings of dissociation and disconnect. These feelings are often described as a sensation of feeling unreal.

Then, before I knew it, and while I was at work I suffered with my first full blown panic attack. This was a terrifying experience that left me feeling as though I just had to get out of there, so I left work only to experience a second attack within minutes of getting in my car.

A Typical Panic Attack For Me

My panic attacks would come on so quickly, in an instant actually, and no sooner did I feel that first symptom then it would turn into a full blown attack. It would happen within seconds, and once started there was no turning back or stopping the attack until it had run its course.

For me I would usually notice myself getting really hot, especially around my face, neck and ears. Then within moments I'd break out into a sweat and start trembling all over. My heart would race like crazy, and my body would become so tense all over that I'd be trembling on the insides as well out.

It would then seem as though all of my senses would become heightened for a moment but then they would almost fade out, meaning that I would start by hearing a high pitched ringing in my ears, but then couldn't hear anything else at all. My eyesight would also become very dim to the point that I would almost lose my sight, and I'd become so numb all over that it would feel as if I couldn't move.

My mouth would become really dry and I'd find it hard to swallow, and it just felt as though I couldn't keep a grip on how I was feeling. Then it would seem as though all of this would become very speeded up which made no sense at all because at the same time I would feel as though I was paralyzed by fear.

During an attack you experience so many feelings and sensations, yet for me the feeling of disconnect and dissociation would cause me to feel as though I was no longer experiencing anything through my senses at all. It was so overwhelming that I would feel as though I was fading out, or that I was going to disappear, if that makes any sense at all.

Thankfully an attack only ever lasted a matter of minutes which is good because any longer and I probably would have passed out. It's almost as if you are literally being taken to the brink of death, as if someone is holding you over the edge of a cliff and threatening to let you go, and you are so terrified that you are pleading for it to stop. And then, as if it was some sick or cruel joke you'd get pulled back to safety, and just like that the panic attack would stop. It's that terrifying.

The whole thing is so crazy, and encompasses your body mind and soul, but luckily, your body cannot maintain all this craziness for too long so it suddenly just stops. It is over in a matter of minutes, quite quickly really although it feels as though it's taking forever when you are having one. And they are certainly long enough to cause you to wonder if you can survive it.

No wonder so many people who suffer with panic attacks actually think they are going to die, as while you are in the middle of one it feels that way.

For Me, My Symptoms Combined With The Intense Feelings Of Dissociation And Disconnect Would Often Leave Me Feeling As Though I Was Going To Fade Out, Or Disappear. If That Makes Any Sense At All!

The Misdiagnosis That Turned A Panic Attack Into A Panic Disorder

After that first attack at work I went straight home, and although I was relieved to have gotten there in one piece, I was petrified that it could happen again. I felt awful, I felt exhausted and I felt scared. I was tense and trembling all over to the point that it felt as though my insides were trembling too. And every time I got up to move, turn around, or even look down I felt so dizzy that I had to grab a hold of something.

A million thoughts started racing through my head as I tried to figure out why this had happened that day. I was fearful of not knowing what was wrong with me, and equally as scared that it might happen again. But perhaps what was bothering me even more was the fact that if it did happen again that I would actually have to tell someone.

Since I had never heard of anything like this before, I wondered if I was suffering with something out of the ordinary, and these thoughts caused me to become fearful of what I might hear if I went to see a doctor. In fact I got so worked up over what it could have been that I couldn't even decided if I should try to get help, or if I should simply wait and hope that it would go away by itself.

The more I thought about it the worse I got. And to make matters even worse I was now also becoming worried that if this was some sort of a mental or emotional disorder, then I would also have to deal with the stigma that went along with it too.

As the symptoms got stronger my fear of hearing a diagnosis were soon outweighed by the fear of what might happen if I didn't get help right away. So I decided to take a chance and try to get some help.

That night, my (now ex) drove me to a walk in clinic where I was met by a tall, well groomed man wearing a long white coat. I felt somewhat relieved by the prospects of finding a resolution, yet I was still completely overwhelmed as a result of what had happened that day. And although I desperately wanted to feel better, I have to admit that I was reluctant to say too much as I wasn't sure if a person could actually get locked up for suffering with such a thing.

Then, as I sat there trying to explain what I had experienced that day, and still feeling quite emotional, I told the doctor everything. Then the moment I paused to take a deep breath, he blurted out his diagnosis. He took one last stern look at me sitting on the table trembling, then he whipped out his prescription pad, scribbled down a prescription and handed it to me. And in that moment he announced it, "You're Pregnant!". And with no further discussion or explanation at all as to why I could possibly be feeling this awful, he turned around and walked right back out through the door.

Now as crazy and unbelievable as this may sound, I soon heard and read about similar stories of other women who had been treated in the same way. Needless to say this visit to the doctor failed to provide me with any sort of relief. In fact I actually ended up feeling ten times worse because now not only did I still have all of the symptoms, but I was also worried about the fact that I still didn't know what was wrong. And that gave me even more to worry about.

I wondered why the doctor hadn't told me what was wrong with me. And I considered the fact that maybe it was because I was suffering with something so bizarre, that no one had actually ever heard about anything like this before. And then if that was the case, perhaps there was no known cure for it either. But then again, maybe he thought that I had something so radically wrong with me that he simply didn't want to have to be the one to tell me, and if that was true, then maybe it could have possibly been untreatable too. Oh my Gawd, how bad can this be? Could I have been suffering with something that could in fact kill you?

I'm sure there are millions of people who suffer with anxiety and panic attacks who would read this and either laugh, or at least feel relieved because they would be able to identify with these thoughts. And they'd probably be thinking something like, "oh my gawd, I'm not the only one who thinks these awful crazy things" because people with anxiety often do end up thinking this way. And even though they are usually very aware of the how these scary thoughts can and do make the whole problem ten times worse, these thoughts go through their minds anyway.

This is why I think it is so incredibly important to recognize and understand the symptoms. If people actually understood what was wrong with them right from the start, why they felt the way they did, and how they came to suffer with this anxiety, the problem would probably start to resolve itself right away. They would no longer have to worry about all of the unanswered questions that would be causing more fear, and this would allow them to focus on getting well instead.

When You Feel Ill You Can Usually Explain How You Feel. When You Are In Pain, You Usually Know Where The Pain Is, When You Suffer With Anxiety There Are So Many Symptoms And Sensations Throughout Your Entire Body That There Is Really Only One Word To Explain It -And That Word Would Be.... Terrifying

The following day I went back to work even though the symptoms were intense and constant. And to make matters worse I was also worried about the fact that I still didn't know what was going on with me, and wondered if it could happen again. I was feeling so stressed and anxious that I soon became completely overwhelmed and I just couldn't stay any longer. I left work to go home.

I actually drove directly to another walk in clinic where I got a similar response to the night before, only this time I did not get a diagnosis of being pregnant, but a simple diagnosis of having stress. In fact over the next two weeks I visited several other doctors only to receive the same response. One by one, they each announced that I was suffering with stress before handing me a new prescription, but not one of these doctors gave me any sort of explanation as to what this meant. I still did not know why this had happened nor did I know what to expect, and I had not received any sort of advice as to what I needed to do in order to get better. Consequently my symptoms continued to get worse.

Two weeks into my ordeal, I was so stressed that I just couldn't go back to work, because no sooner would I get there and I would have to turn around and leave. I couldn't sleep, I couldn't eat and I was so tense and dizzy all of the time that I constantly felt bewildered and numb. I was constantly anxious and worried and the only thing that gave me any sort of relief from these feelings were the intermittent panic attacks which I was now experiencing several times a day.

I had gotten to the point where I could no longer go out on my own without having a panic attack, and if I did, it would literally leave me feeling paralysed by fear. In fact I had reached a point where I was no longer really living my life but instead I was merely existing.

Since I couldn't possibly continue to work I had to quit my job. This meant that I was now unemployed and was turning down social invitations and opportunities that I would have otherwise loved to have accepted. Within a matter of weeks I had gone from being an outgoing, happy-go-lucky social butterfly to becoming someone who not even I could recognize. In a nutshell, I had basically become a recluse in my home and was avoiding everyone in my life.

The Intensity Of My Panic Attacks Were Usually Debilitating To Say The Very Least.

For anyone who has suffered with anxiety and panic attacks they will be able to identify with what I am saying. For those of you who have not had the misfortune, you would probably find this all very hard to believe. But the truth is that if you knew me now, or knew me before this happened to me, you would never in a million years believe that something like this could possibly happen to someone like me. The scary thing is that it can also happen to you!

The sad news is that knowing what I know now, I truly believe that had any of those doctors spent even five minutes explaining what stress was, why I was experiencing those symptoms, what to possibly expect next, or what I needed to do in order to overcome this, I truly believe that my symptoms would never in a million years have gotten anywhere near as bad as they did. Nor would I have ended up suffering with anxiety, chronic panic attacks or agoraphobia.

For me, as with so many other people, it was not just the stress and panic that was creating my problems, but it was the not knowing what was wrong with me that made these problems get worse. In the end it was the fear about the fear, which ultimately made the whole experience blow up into a full blown panic disorder.

The consequences of not being diagnosed properly or having these symptoms explained to me meant that this whole experience caused me to become agoraphobic. This left me in a state where I could no longer even do the most simple and normal things that I had always done. And I'm talking about things like taking my dog for a walk, getting in my car to drive to the store or even walking around to the front of my house to get the mail out of the mailbox. Because if I did I suffered with another panic attack and this would cause me to literally become paralyzed by fear.

I Truly Believe That Had I Been Diagnosed With Anxiety When I First Went To See A Doctor, And Had Someone Actually Taken The Time To Explain The Symptoms And Why I Was Suffering With This, My Anxiety Would Never Have Gotten So Out Of Control. And That I Probably Would Have Started My Recovery Right There And Then.

By the way I am still baffled as to why that first doctor gave me the prescription for anti-anxiety pills if he thought I was pregnant. I still haven't figured out if the pills were supposed to have been for me or were they meant for the baby? Oh by the way, no I wasn't pregnant.

Searching For Answers

For the longest time it seemed that my symptoms continued to get worse, and that was in spite of the fact that I would have done anything just to have gotten better. I had no luck with getting help from any of the doctors I had seen, and was now walking around with a couple of bottles of pills and about four additional prescriptions in my purse. I wasn't having any luck finding answers, so I came to the conclusion that I was going to have to take matters into my own hands so that I could figure out what was going on with me, and hopefully find a cure.

Since all this started back in the 90s and we didn't have the internet at the time, the options for finding information were nowhere near as easy as what they are today. In fact, the only real option available was to buy self help books, so I got myself over to the UBC bookstore where I bought every book I could find on the subject. Then, like so many others who have been in the same boat as I was in, I returned home and started to fill out all of the questionnaires.

Take my advice on this one; don't waste your money on buying a whole bunch of books on anxiety that pretty much all say the same thing. Although I am not a doctor or considered to be an expert in this area I would suggest that all you need to know and understand are the symptoms so that you can recognize which ones you are suffering with, and enough information to arm yourself with the right questions to ask any doctors or therapists you may work with. Then put the books down and turn your focus to how you are going to overcome it, and put your time and effort into that instead.

Most people I have ever met who have suffered with anxiety and panic attacks have done exactly the same thing as I did, and that meant that they went out and bought as many books on the subject that they could find. In fact, I've coached some stress management clients who have shown up with a gym bag full of text books on the subject only to feel doomed by their findings in the books.

It is human nature to want to know what is wrong with you, especially when you feel so out of sorts, and I am 100% on board with being proactive. However, one of the dangers of filling out all of these questionnaires and inventories is that a lot of them go into detail about your personal and family history. This will mean that you are almost guaranteed to identify with at least some of the questions, which could then lead you to believe that your stress is hereditary. Then not only might you end up believing that it is hereditary (which may in fact be "part" of the problem) but you may then also buy into the idea that if it is, then you probably won't be able to overcome it.

This to me was so disheartening to read and hear, and can actually become a further cause of anxiety. That sort of doom and gloom can make anyone depressed, not to mention the fact that while you are wallowing in this negative information, you will probably fail to recognize the real reason that you became stressed in the first place. And this can become a real roadblock which could prevent you from getting well.

Very often when this happens a person may feel that they will have to live with this forever, and that is not necessarily the case. Not only that, but as long as you are focusing on the problem, and the causes, (which things like family history may or may not have contributed to) you are not focusing on getting well instead. And this can only make matters worse.

Also if you get caught up in doing some of these inventories you run the risk of not only diagnosing yourself with every mental illness under the sun, but you could end up diagnosing everyone else in your family too. And this will only justify why you have this problem. This way of thinking can keep you stuck.

While reading these books I realized that I could have diagnosed myself with having anxiety, panic attacks, depression, multiple personality disorder, ADD, manic depressive disorder, bipolar, PTSD and just about every other condition you can think of. Oh, other than being pregnant that is. Hmmm, kinda makes me wonder if that guy in the long white coat was a real doctor after all.

Unfortunately, I also kept getting the very same advice from the therapists I had seen back then as what I had also found in some of these books. And that was that the anxiety is probably just a part of who you are, and that you might as well get used to it, or that you should just accept it. And I was constantly being told that the best way to get over my anxiety was to just get out there and do whatever it was that I wanted to do, then hopefully if I did it often enough the anxiety should eventually just subside.

I found this all to be very disheartening, but I just kept thinking to myself, and saying to these therapists, "This is ridiculous, how could this possibly be a part of who I am, I never had this thing before and I certainly don't want it now". I was desperate to overcome this anxiety and yet I was constantly hearing and reading that it just might not be possible.

Obviously these books were written by people who had no idea what it is like to suffer with anxiety, because what they seemed to fail to understand was that not only do most people who suffer with these disorders desperately want to get their life back. But the very thing they need in order to do so is to get rid of the symptoms first.

When Your Symptoms Are So Intense That You Feel As Though You Are Going To Die The Last Thing You Want To Hear Is That You Just Need To Go Out And Face Your Fears

My Turning Point -From Mission Impossible To Mission Possible

By now I was desperate to get my life back. From what I had read and from the experiences I had had while in therapy I was starting to feel doomed, and wondered if I would ever have my life back again. And although I was starting to consider what options I had to run some sort of business from home so that I would never have to leave the house again, I was also becoming more and more determined to overcome this.

As I said earlier, I just kept thinking that I had never had this thing before, and I certainly didn't want it now. And the more frustrated I got with the whole situation the more determined I got as well. I started to feel that it wasn't going to be good enough to just get my life back the way it had been before, but I wanted to become even stronger. I wanted to become more confident, more empowered and more courageous. I wanted to overcome any fears, phobias, obstacles or objections that might have potentially held me back in the past, and I wanted to become the best version of myself possible. I had actually reached a point where I decided that I wanted to become unstoppable.

After Suffering With Anxiety And Panic Attacks For Several Years I Finally Resigned Myself To The Fact That I Would Probably Never Work Outside Of My Home Again. As Time Went On The Thought Of Ever Having Any Resemblance Of Normal Life Was Becoming More Of A Dream.

A New Approach To Outsmarting Stress

After visiting doctors and therapists and reading every book I could find on anxiety, panic attacks and agoraphobia and still not having experienced any sort of relief, I started to look into alternative options. And since I was desperate I was willing to try anything.

By now I seemed to have a very good understanding of what stress, anxiety and panic attacks were, and yet I still didn't know why I was suffering with them. Nor had I found anything that offered me any sort of relief.

I started by visiting a health food store where I loaded up on all sorts of herbs and aromatherapy products which offered as many promises as there were remedies, but it seemed that I was still experiencing very little relief. In all fairness to these products, I now realize that it can take a while for many of the natural remedies to kick in, and that there are some which are invaluable when it comes to managing stress.

So I kept looking and trying new things, and continued to search for new ways to overcome this until I finally came across a couple of therapies that piqued my interest. Two of the most important ones were NLP and TFT

I started out by attending a free talk on NLP and loved the concept, although I wasn't' completely sure if it would help me overcome my anxiety. But after experiencing how NLP could be used to change the way we think and feel I decided to sign up for the practitioner training. This allowed me to learn so many of the exercises and processes of NLP, and I was so intrigued that I also signed up for the Master Practitioner Course.

By now I had come to realize that there are many aspects to suffering with anxiety. And as I was learning these exercises I could see how some of them could be applied to some of the individual aspects of anxiety. And it was through experimenting in this way that I started to experience some positive results, and I finally saw that there was hope.

As luck would have it I also came across a Psychologist in Vancouver who was working with a lot of New Age type therapies such as visualization, hypnosis and a new therapy called Thought Field Therapy. He was getting some amazing results, and at the time referred to himself as a recovering psychologist as much of his efforts and successes were a result of these New Age models. I immediately booked an appointment with him, and while there I had my first experience with Thought Field Therapy.

At first I wasn't sure what to think as couldn't see how it would work, but when the session ended and I left his office I decided to go for a walk. Instead of getting straight back into my car I started walking up the street, and for the first time in years I was walking alone on a busy street in downtown Vancouver and I didn't feel anxious at all.

However, even though I was so excited to have finally found something that helped to relieve the symptoms, and I was feeling much more relaxed than I had felt in years, a little voice in my head kept reminding me that I shouldn't go any further. Even though I felt like I just wanted to keep on walking and that I could have walked for miles, this little voice kept warning me that if I went too far, I could have had another panic attack and I wouldn't be able to get back to my car. So reluctantly, I stopped walking and turned around and went back to my car instead. I felt so torn between defying the little voice, and playing it safe, but I knew that going back to my car was the safest thing to do.

Herein lays another huge problem when you have suffered with anxiety, panic attacks and agoraphobia. In order to function in a somewhat normal way, and for the sake of self motivation, we often put very strict limits on ourselves and our lives. These limits may include things like how far we think we can go away from our safe place, or what things we think we are, or are not, now capable of doing. We then internalize these limits as being real and develop some new limiting beliefs about ourselves and our capabilities. These new beliefs become so ingrained and so believable that we take them on as a part of our identity, and then sadly we go through life unconsciously living up to them.

As luck would have it this psychologist was about to teach Thought Field Therapy to a group of doctors, psychologists and counsellors in Vancouver, so I enrolled in to the course. I probably got more out of that training than anyone else did, because not only did I get to train in an amazing therapy but I also got to experience firsthand how powerful it can be. And because I believed in this method so much, I continued on to do the advanced training before repeating the training several times over again.

However, even though I was finally experiencing some relief as a result of using these therapies, I realized that neither the Thought Field Therapy nor the NLP would work well enough alone to combat the anxiety as a whole, or at least not for me. So I started to experiment with the different processes and combined exercises from NLP, TFT and some additional New Age and alternative therapies, as well as making some major changes in my life and I soon completely overcome my anxiety, panic attacks and agoraphobia.

Although it took me a while, the results were amazing and I finally fully recovered from these debilitating disorders which had kept me a prisoner in my own home for many years. And that is how I also came to develop some pretty amazing programs to help people like you prevent, and overcome your stresses too.

The Stress And Burnout Awareness and Prevention Guide (Book)

The Stress And Burnout Awareness and Prevention Program (Workshop – live and online)

Tapping Into Your Mind Body Magic

1st Key To Managing Stress – Learn How To Recognize The Symptoms

Recognizing The Symptoms Of Stress

Change In Sleeping Or Eating Habits

Tension – Especially In The Neck, Jaw, Shoulders And Around The Eyes

Headaches, Irritability, Tired

Pessimistic Outlook, Easily Upset, Hypersensitive

Overwhelmed

Negative Self Talk And Negative Thoughts

Problems Concentrating

Obsessive Thinking

Avoiding Social Situations

Feeling Blue

Learning How To Recognize The Symptoms Of Stress Could Prompt You To Take The Right Action At The Right Time. This Action Could Prevent Your Stress From Manifesting Into Anxiety, Panic Attacks Or Agoraphobia.

NOTES

Recognizing The Symptoms Of Anxiety

When suffering with anxiety, in addition to the symptoms of stress you may also experience:

Trembling – Internally And Externally – Visibly Shaking

Muscle Tension

Dry Mouth

Shortness Of Breath

Heart Palpitations

Feeling Light Headed

Feeling Dissociated Or Unreal

Sweaty Or Clammy Hands

Feeling Helpless, Hopeless Or Fearful

If Our Body Is Our Temple, Then To Suffer With Anxiety, Panic Attacks, Depression And Agoraphobia Is More Like Living In The Temple Of Doom.

NOTES

Recognizing The Symptoms Of Panic Attacks

Anxiety may be accompanied by panic attacks. These attacks are much more violent on the body and may include the following symptoms

Feeling Faint

Chest Pain Or Tightness In The Chest

Shaking

Sweating

Nausea

Numbness Or Tingling In The Face, Hands, Legs

Stomach Upset

Feeling Paralysed By Fear

Flushed – Very Hot, Chilled or Both

Feeling As Though You Will Choke

Fear of Losing Control Or That You Are Going To Die

NOTES

Any Sensation Which Replicates A Single Symptom Which You May Have Experienced When Having A Panic Attack, Such As Suddenly Getting Warm Because The Sun Pops It's Head Out From Behind A Cloud, Has The Potential, And The Power To Ignite Yet Another Panic Attack.

NOTES

What Is Agoraphobia?

The true meaning of agoraphobia is a fear of the market place. In other words a fear of wide open spaces, although the spaces do not necessarily have to be that open. From someone who suffered with it for ten years I can tell you firsthand what it is, how it can develop, and the impact it can have on your life. In my program Tapping Into Your Mind Body Magic I also teach the methods and tools which I personally used to overcome my ten year stint with panic attacks and agoraphobia.

For those of you who like to get a little more personal, I have also made a couple of videos where I, along with a friend of mine who is a well respected psychiatrist talk about anxiety, panic attacks and agoraphobia.

Agoraphobia - In My Own Words

Agoraphobia is an intense fear of having a panic attack, losing control, or doing something crazy while a) either outside in a public place, or b) too far away from your point of safety (usually your home, or possibly your car). This fear is usually initiated by the intense feelings and symptoms of anxiety, panic and fear, and can cause someone to become fearful of public places and avoid going outside altogether.

There are varying degrees of agoraphobia and it can develop so quickly and easily for those who suffer with anxiety and panic attacks. Knowing how to recognize the symptoms, understanding how this can manifest and develop, and learning how to manage your stress could protect you from ever having this happen to you.

How Does Agoraphobia Develop?

If you have been reading this book you will know that I personally suffered with anxiety and panic attacks which literally brought my life to a standstill, and I suffered with this for about ten years. If you know me now, or you knew me before I had this debilitating experience you would have a hard time believing this to be true. It would be difficult for most people to imagine that something like this could affect someone like me. But the truth is that it can happen to absolutely anyone, and it can come on so suddenly and aggressively that it can hit you before you even know it. So be forewarned and take my advice, arm yourself by becoming aware of the symptoms. And please, spread the word.

Agoraphobia has the potential to develop as a result of experiencing panic attacks or certain phobias which could cause people to either avoid certain situations, or prevent them from living an otherwise normal life which would also include going out to public places.

The types of phobias I am talking about may include fears or phobias of bridges, elevators, flying, going in a car, driving on a highway, or going into stores or high rises, just to name a few. The reason why these phobias can develop into something more serious is because phobias such as these have the capacity to permeate into other areas of your life.

For example, claustrophobia which is a fear of small spaces may cause someone to avoid going into an elevator; this could then develop into a fear of heights which would be brought on by the fear of going up more than a few floors in an elevator. The fear of heights along with the claustrophobia could then develop into a fear of flying and this could then permeate into a fear of travelling too far. Also the fear of heights could then develop into a fear of crossing bridges or even going up a mountain.

On the other hand the fear of heights could cause a person to avoid driving across a bridge, which could then manifest into a fear of driving anywhere, or even getting into a car. And the cycle can go on until it permeates into what may seem to be unrelated parts of your life, and this can become quite limiting to say the least. This is also when there is a potential to develop agoraphobia.

Agoraphobia As A Result Of Panic Attacks I Will Tell You My Story

Agoraphobia will often develop for a person who suffers with panic attacks as a result of the panic attack happening outdoors and creating a negative anchor which can then become associated with a place or situation where the panic attack previously occurred. For instance, I experienced my first panic attack at work and then had another later that day when I was driving home. This made me worry that it could happen again if I went back to work, not to mention the fear of it happening again when I was driving.

It is typical for someone to develop the fear of having another panic attack in a place or situation where one has already occurred, and it may only take one or two attacks while driving before someone will want to avoid driving all together.

Part of the problem with having panic attacks is not just the attacks themselves, but the accompanying thoughts of not being able to escape from wherever you are at the time you have the attack. Being trapped in a car in a traffic jam and not being able to flee to safety will create more intense fears and will likely bring on another attack.

Now your fear of having another panic attack may also be accompanied by the fear of not being able to escape from whatever situation you are in at the time of the attack. And on top of that, you might also worry about doing something crazy in order to distract yourself, or to get away from the situation you are in if you have an attack. Many people who suffer with panic attacks worry that they might do something like abandon their car to run to safety, run out in front of an oncoming car and cause an accident, or even do something as irrational as jump off a bridge, if that is where they were at the time of an attack.

I'm sure that this is all very hard to believe for anyone who has never experienced anything like this before, and I know most people would wonder why anyone would be thinking such crazy thoughts to begin with. But the truth is that it is often not the thoughts that will set off another panic attack, but it can be the feelings themselves that are brought on by the fears, that will ignite another attack. This is how panic attacks and agoraphobia can spiral out of control and turn into a debilitating disorder.

The fear of having an attack and not being able to get to safety can turn a simple task such standing in a line-up in a grocery store or bank, sitting in a restaurant eating or in hair salon getting your hair done, or standing waiting for the light to change for you to cross the street, into a terrifying experience. These thoughts and feelings could come on at anytime you feel trapped and can literally cause an agoraphobic person to feel immobilized, to the point of becoming literally paralyzed by fear.

As I'm sure you can imagine it would only take going through such an experience a few times where you feel that you cannot get back to safety, to want to limit the distances you'll travel away from your home or your place of safety. These distances can become so short that many people with agoraphobia literally cannot leave their home no matter how much they would love to go out. And some are even so terrified that they can become confined to a particular room in their home and in extreme cases they may even be confined to a piece of furniture.

Agoraphobia Has The Ability To Turn You Into A Prisoner Within Your Own Home. Some Even End Up Confining Themselves To A Single Room While Others May Even Confine Themselves To A Single Piece Of Furniture.

NOTES

How Could It Be Possible For Us To Not Recognize These Symptoms?

With so many symptoms which are undeniably uncomfortable and obvious, you would think that it wouldn't be possible to overlook them. But in reality recognizing our own stress is often not as easy as you would think, and that is why more often than not it goes undetected or undiagnosed until it is too late. Here are a few reasons why we fail to recognize the warning signs that we could be suffering with stress and anxiety.

As you can see from these lists the symptoms of stress and anxiety are very physiological, and yet stress is often considered to be a mental or emotional problem. This can cause us to overlook any physical symptoms which may have been caused by stress and simply write them off as being caused by something totally different. For instance, tension in your back or neck could be symptoms of stress, however if we don't realize that we are stressed we may simply assume that the tension has been caused by the fact that we are not sitting or sleeping in the right position.

Stress is also such an ambiguous word that is often so over used and misunderstood that we fail to see what other emotions could be causing us to feel bad. For instance someone who is sad or angry may get these emotions confused with being stressed, but in reality, they may simply be just sad or angry. However not identifying these individual emotions or what is causing them to raise their heads, can leave them to fester and become quite overwhelming.

Following is an observation I made years ago when I first moved to Canada. No matter where I was or who I was talking to it appeared that everyone believed that they were suffering stress. I remember clients telling me in the hair salon about their stress, and I also heard a group of kids on the bus discussing how stressed out they were. I have to admit, I didn't even know what this meant, I knew that it had something to do with being under pressure but the way that this word was being thrown around made me think that it had to mean something else. Besides, even with my interpretation of what stress was I still couldn't understand how most of these people could consider themselves to be stressed.

I had never heard the word stress being thrown around in Britain the way that it was in North America, so I had to do a bit of research. But even after reading up on it, it still didn't make any sense to me why so many people failed to identify individual emotions and their causes but instead considered themselves to be stressed.

Then after experiencing my own anxiety and panic attack and becoming fully aware of what stress was, I came to the realization that it seemed to be an ambiguous word that was being used to include so many individual feelings and emotions. In other words, I saw "stress" as being like this huge cloud of emotions that nobody could quite put their finger on.

The problem which I saw with this interpretation was that it kept people from first identifying what was really bothering them, as in which emotion, and secondly, what had caused the individual emotion in the first place.

Looking back I realized that if a person identified an individual emotion as opposed to thinking that they were stressed, they would then more easily be able to identify what caused the emotion and resolve it. For example, if I was to say I am stressed out, it is as if I am only aware of all of the symptoms. However, if I was to say I am worried, then I can easily determine what I am worried about. And in turn, I could try to find a solution to the thing that caused me to worry. Or, the same would go if I was angry. By knowing which emotion is bothering you will allow you to then identify why you are experiencing it in this particular moment in time.

A friend of mine who is a psychologist recently told me that he was going to start taking anti depressants. I asked why, and he answered by saying that he was stressed and depressed, and then went on to tell me that he couldn't understand why because of all of the things that were working in his life. After he listed them off, I then asked him, "well what is missing in your life?" And bingo! He said that he was lonely and wanted to meet someone to spend his life with. So my point is, is he really "stressed" and in need of medication, or is he actually "lonely" and in need of finding a girlfriend?

Now that we had an answer to what was really causing him to feel bad we could come up with a solution to put him out of his misery. It was much easier to find a quick solution because we had identified the real cause and emotion instead of having him walk around in a cloud of "stress" popping anti depressant pills for the rest of his life.

Another reason that we often fail to recognize that we are under a great deal of stress is because we don't always see how the events in our lives affect how we feel. Even when something upsetting happens and we are aware that we feel emotionally upset we still don't necessarily recognize how the event caused us to become stressed.

Also, when we under severe stress we usually feel so overwhelmed by the problem that we can't think straight, and certainly not clearly enough to figure out what is really going on. By becoming aware of which feelings and emotions we are experiencing and by cluing in to what has actually caused the emotions to flare up in the first place, we can find a solution and put an end to our stress.

It is often said that South Americans live in their bodies, and that North Americas live in their heads. This means that we North Americans are typically not that aware of our feelings, our energy or our intuitions. Therefore we may not necessarily recognize our physical symptoms until they become severe. Then, to make matters worse we often make the mistake of trying to rationalize what is going on in our minds, instead of paying attention to, and being aware of what our bodies are trying to tell us.

One Of The Reasons That We Often Don't Recognize That We Are Suffering With Stress Is Because So Many Of The Symptoms Are Physical, And Yet Stress Is Often Considered To Be A Mental Or Emotional Problem Of The Mind

Recognizing, Diagnosing And Relieving Stress -The Missing Link

The more I got to experience the panic and anxiety the more I realized that it is a very physical experience. And it was this realization that brought into my awareness the reasons why so many people fail to recognize when they are under stress.

There are two major factors that prevent us from recognizing that we are stressed. The first being that stress is usually considered to be, and is looked at as a mental or emotional problem, and yet so many of the symptoms which we experience when stressed or anxious are actually physical. So we often don't realize that our physical symptoms are caused by stress. And secondly, we fail to realize what in our lives are the real causes of our stress.

It also made me realize how our thoughts really affect our physical feelings, and in a nutshell that we humans are in fact mind body entities. Knowing this then it only made sense to me that it would be well worth considering, and trying mind body therapies to try to overcome this.

What Do I Mean By Saying That We Are Mind Body Entities?

Consider this. Every thought whether positive or negative will elicit a certain set of feelings. This means that everything that we experience in life is a mind body experience. If we *think* about a certain thing then it will elicit, or bring about certain *feelings*. And, if we *feel* a certain way, then these *feelings* will generate associated *thoughts*. There is no getting around this as it is a fact of life.

We are mind/body entities, living in a physical bodies, but we, especially in the Western Culture have been trained to *think* (sometimes way too much) with our minds. And in turn are discouraged from allowing ourselves to trust our *feelings,* being our physical feelings and our intuitions. But I believe that we need to consider both – always!

I like to *think* of it this way. We *think* with our conscious mind, our brain or in our heads, whichever way you want to see it. And we *feel* throughout our body or our subconscious mind.

Feelings are about energy, flow and freedom. *Thought* is about vision, imagination and planning. *Thoughts* can be very powerful, but when used alone they can also be very restrictive. *Feelings* can bring integrity to our *thoughts* and can be a real driving force.

We need to allow our *thoughts* and our *feelings* to work together in harmony, after all this is reality.

Our thoughts and feelings work well as a team; however in our western culture we have often been trained to ignore our *feelings*, putting way too much emphasis on *thoughts*. (Hey it is easier to control people this way) This then supports the notion that many of us in the western culture spend way too much time living in our heads. And yet in order to live life to the fullest and experience what is really important to us, we need to live in our bodies as well. And perhaps more importantly, we need to be willing to experience our feelings and pay attention to our intuitions.

I have often heard coaches and motivators tell people not to allow their feelings to get in the way of making decisions. But it is my opinion that this could potentially be a huge mistake, because all too often it will be our feelings which will steer us in the right direction. And considering it is all but impossible to separate our thoughts from our feelings it might not be so easy to do.

We have been and often still are taught to primarily use our heads, to think, strategize, plan, and analyze our lives. But we also need to pay attention to our feelings too. Excerpt from New

Year Resolutions, Goals, Dreams and Aspirations *by* Suzanne J. Price – on planning and achieving goals.

We Are Mind Body Entities Living In A World Where We In North America And The Western Cultures Have Been Brainwashed Into Focusing Way Too Much On What Is Going On In Our Heads And Not Paying Attention To What Is Going On In Our Bodies

So What Has This Got To Do With Stress And How It Can Manifest In Our Bodies?

As I already explained, stress is a mind body experience. Here is a simplistic explanation of how stress and or a fear can develop and manifest into physical symptoms in the body, and cause us to experience some of the symptoms when under stress, or faced with fear or anxiety.

First imagine water running through a hose pipe. Then imagine that the hose pipe gets a kink in it. What happens? The water flow is cut off and can no longer run freely through the hose.

The fear response in the body works in very much the same way. We have life energy flowing through our body on a continuous basis, much like the water running through the hose. When we encounter a fear or a negative emotional situation, for instance let's say that something frightens us,, then it would be as if there is a disruption or a block in the energy flow. This would have the same effect as if the hose pipe got a kink in it, and is known as an energy disruption.

When you experience such an energy disruption, meaning your energy can no longer flow easily, your energy force plummets. Depending on the intensity of the fear, your physical energy can drop by up to 80% (you might recall watching a movie where someone was being told about a tragic event and the bearer of the bad news would say "you might want to sit down, I have some bad news").

Also, your brain hemispheres lose communication with each other (ever wonder why you can't think straight while in a stressful situation?) And the "fight or flight" response may kick in, meaning that you will experience all of the symptoms of the stress response. Excerpt from, How To Turn That First Glance Into A Date, *by* Suzanne J. Price – on dating and the fear of rejection.

Can you see now how stress is in fact a mind body experience? If so, then it would really make no sense to think of stress as only being a mental or emotional problem? And if you agree, then I'm sure that you will also be able to see the rationale behind the idea of treating stress on a mind body level.

Prevention

Remember stress can and does manifest into anxiety, panic attacks, burnout and agoraphobia. And by now you may have already noticed that you might even fall into one of the categories that make up the statistics about stress. Don't be fooled by the mindset that this only happens to other people, and don't let stress take over *your* life.

To avoid becoming a statistic of one of the more acute forms of stress start paying attention to your symptoms, and commit to living a lifestyle that will help keep stress at bay. Remember, awareness is the key to prevention.

Now that you have a good understanding of what stress is, how to recognize the symptoms, and how they can manifest into more debilitating disorders, I am going to point out some of the major causes of stress in people's lives. It is surprising to note that many of the real underlying causes of stress go undetected, and after reading this I'm sure you will understand why. Awareness is the key to preventing your stress from ever manifesting into anything other than just that, Stress!

The truth is that we cannot avoid stress. Even if you are financially wealthy and you spend your days sitting at home relaxing by your pool, the chances are that you could still experience stress. In fact if you do live your life in such a way you will stand a very good chance of becoming stressed as a result of boredom, and may end up feeling as though you have no passion, purpose or meaning in your life. You may simply be unfulfilled. So no matter what you do in life, without the right awareness there may be no escaping the effects of stress.

So with that said then the next best thing is to learn how to identify the possible stressors in your life.

2nd Key To Managing Stress – Learn How To Recognize The Real Stressors In Your Life

The next step to preventing stress from manifesting into anything more serious is to become aware of what could potentially be the causes of stress in your own life. Knowing this will give you the power to make positive changes.

There are two major groups of events that could cause stress. The first one being that you have experienced some sort of unexpected or tragic event in your life which may even potentially be life altering. And the second being that you have been experiencing some sort of ongoing, underlying issue that you may, or may not have identified as being a cause of stress.

In most cases when we have suffered with some sort of unexpected or tragic event we would, without a doubt, be very aware of how it has affected us. When stress is a result of such an experience and if the symptoms are acute enough, as in you are experiencing intense physical, mental and emotional distress, you could even be suffering with a condition called Post Traumatic Stress Disorder.

If on the other hand your stress is a result of some sort of ongoing underlying issue that you may or may not have identified as being a problem, then you may find that you will suffer the effects and symptoms of stress even if you don't recognize what is causing it.

As I mentioned earlier, part of the reason why this can happen is because it is not always obvious how a problem can have such a negative impact on our lives. And secondly we may simply be focussing on the wrong issue. Here are a few good examples.

After I had recovered from my anxiety and panic attack I was coaching a client who was pretty much in the same stressed out state that I had been in. I could certainly identify with what she was going through.

As we discuss what was causing her stress she explained to me that it was the pressures of having to find day care, having to rely on her aging mother to help look after her child, and having constant run-ins with her husband over not being home when the child finished school in the afternoons, not having enough family time, and seldom eating meals together. When talking about her work she immediately assured me that she loved her job and that it had been the one stable thing in her life, as she had been with the same company for many years.

However, after asking her a few more questions about her job, I soon found out that she was in fact working in undesirable working conditions. Also, she actually didn't particularly like the work, she had to work very long hours and that she had also taken a pay cut due to the economy. The one thing that she kept telling me was that her employers really needed her and that they depended on her so much that she just couldn't let them down.

For her, because she was focussing on all of the problems which stemmed from the fact that she was working in this job, being the daycare and family issues, she had failed to see that it was the job itself, and her beliefs and fears around letting these people down that was the real cause of the stress. And although she had suffered with this debilitating stress for several years, the mere fact that we had now pinpointed what was really causing it turned out to be enough for her to experience some immediate relief.

The next thing we did was discuss the option of her quitting her job, in which case, she was able to do, so I coached her through that process. For her, the realization of what was really causing her stress and the decision to quit lifted such a weight off her shoulders that her anxiety literally disappeared in that moment in time. It was like watching an immediate transformation.

This lack of awareness of where the real stress is coming from, or the inability to make such a decision can keep you stuck for years, in fact it can be immobilizing. Yet, this lack of awareness or the habit of defending the position that you are in, is not that uncommon at all.

To be honest my stress stemmed from a similar thing. Only for me I was blaming the job and failing to realize that I was working there because my now "ex" was someone who was terrified of my independence.

To me it seemed that it was the job that was causing my stress. And since I had been self employed for many years and had been used to having a lot of control over my time, I did find the job stifling. So I thought it was just the job which was my cause of stress.

However, the reason that I was working there in the first place was because of my ex's insecurities. Every time I talked about starting my own business again he would say that he wanted to get married and buy a house, so he would convince me to stick with the job for the sake of getting a mortgage. Or he would suggest moving to California so I should wait until we decided where we were going to live. There were many other excuses that kept cropping up which caused me to keep putting my life on hold, and stay in a job that I didn't like.

My point is that in the long run although I hated that job, the underling stress was created by an unsupportive relationship for which I kept putting my life on hold for. As I literally gave up my own goals, dreams in an effort to please someone else.

I'm sure that you can see in both of these examples how easy it can be to get sidetracked from the real cause of stress. We can actually become so consumed by the problems which have been created by the stress that we end up missing, or ignoring the warning signs that created the stress in the first place.

Following is a list of some of the ongoing issues that people experience in life that can become a major cause of stress. Recognizing which issues cause stress in your own life will give you the power to make positive changes.

Money And Financial Issues

Loneliness And Lack Of Connection

Disconnect From Community

A Lack Of Family Support Or Partnership With A Significant Other

Career

Relationships

Lack Of Friends

Weak Social Or Family Structure

Health Issues

Bad Habits

Monumental Events Such As Family Rituals Including Birthdays And Seasonal Holidays Like Christmas

School Or University

Unsupportive Living Or Working Environment

Boredom

Feeling That You Have No Power Or Control Over Your Life

Feeling Trapped In A Situation That You Cannot Leave

Lack Of Self Awareness

Poor Spiritual Connection

Feeling Helpless Or Hopeless

Feeling Stuck In A Certain Area Of Your Life, Or Feeling Suck In Life In General.

To get out of this rut see – It's Your Life, So What Are You Going To Do With It?

There are so many reasons that could be weighing you down and causing you stress, but unless you identify the real cause and how it is affecting you, you may be stuck for years.

NOTES

3rd Key To Managing Stress – Recognizing What You Do, Or Do Not Have Control To Change In Your Life

We could also divide our stressors into two general groups, being those that we feel are within our control to change, and those that we have no control over changing, or at least not in this moment in time.

Some of the stressors in our life may not be, or may not seem, as though they are within our own power to change, or at least not in the present time. However as long as we are aware of our own personal stressors we will realize that there are many things in our lives that we do have the power change, and life skills and lifestyle fall into this group.

Life skills are essentially behaviours which we learn, often unconsciously throughout our lives. In essence these skills help to make up who we are, or who we become as a person. The tricky thing about life skills is, because we often learn them unconsciously, we are not always aware of how they can have such a positive or negative effect on our lives.

An example of an ineffective life skill would be having poor time management skills. This would mean that you would probably be running late most of the time and this could then cause you to spend much of your time rushing around feeling hurried. As a result you will likely feel stressed and may even become distracted and disorganized, and this in turn could become the reason why you then become even tardier. Our bad habits or poor life skills can take on a life of their own and ultimately spiral out of control

Life skills can essentially make or break you and that is why I feel it is so important to become aware of them from a stress management point of view.

Take a few minutes to think about where in your life you could use some improvement. How are your own personal life skills and habits affecting you? It will pay you to identity if your behaviours help, or hinder the results you get throughout your life.

Your lifestyle can also be a major source of stress, and may include factors such as how well you eat, sleep or pay attention to your body mind and soul. Habits would also fall under lifestyle and may be positive, such as exercising right, practicing spiritually and personal and professional development, or negative, such as eating junk food, drinking too much, smoking or taking drugs.

Even day to day lifestyle habits can make a huge difference to how you experience life and manage stress. For instance if you don't get enough sleep you will eventually feel tired and restless, and a lack of sleep is guaranteed to cause you stress. As will poor eating habits that will have major negative effect on your body, not to mention the impact it could have on your self esteem and possibly even your life. Simply knowing these things puts you into a position of becoming aware that you do have a choice as to how you live your life. The question is, are you ready, willing and able to take that responsibility?

Some Simple Life Lessons That Can Keep Stress At Bay

In this following section I have outlined some every day habits that can become major causes of stress, and I have given some tips on how to prevent them from becoming stressors in your own life.

Slow Down

Other than the danger of hurting ourselves or getting into accidents, constantly rushing around can literally cause us to lose time. We are living in a time and place where everything is so speeded up that we are missing out on whole life experiences, only to regret this in the end.

Slow down, enjoy a stroll, listen to the birds sing, smell the flowers or the ocean, take the time to taste the food that you put into your mouth, feel the sun or the breeze on your skin, watch the sun rise at dawn, and set at dusk, stare at the moon for hours while listening to the waves lap up onto the shore, or spend a rainy day just hanging out with a friend talking, laughing and having fun. Savour every moment that you can.

The crazy thing is that we get so caught up in the rat race that we miss out on so many of the really important things in life, and yet the very reason so many of us get caught up in our crazy lives is because we hope, that one day we will be able to slow down, relax, and enjoy the simpler things in life. This is crazy.

Find Clarity In Your Life And Create Crystal Clear Goals

One of the biggest causes of stress in so many people's lives comes from the fact that they simply feel stuck. They may feel stuck in a particular area of their life, or they may feel suck in life in general. What this often means is that although a person may know that he or she wants change in their life, they may not necessarily know what it is that they want to change, or of what they want instead.

This does not necessarily apply to everyone as there are a lot of people who are very aware of what they would like to change in their life, but they feel that they face too many obstacles. And sadly this could prevent them from ever moving forward.

Some of the more common obstacles which can prevent someone from taking action and changing whatever situation they would like to change may include things like: lack of support, financial difficulties, resistance from others (perhaps parents or significant other), family commitments, or a lack of skills required for the type of change they want to experience. Besides these, some people are also faced with additional obstacles that may be more challenging to overcome, as they include issues such as social, cultural, or religious beliefs, disabilities, or even gender inequality.

Then there are those people who just feel stuck. In fact they may feel so stuck that their only awareness of wanting or needing some sort of change will come from within, and may present itself in the form of an uneasy feeling. These feelings could present themselves in many ways and may include feelings of loneliness, anger, frustration, sadness, or despair. Or a person may simply feel that something is missing from their life, or that they are just not happy. Some of these people may start to wonder what life is all about, or even question whether this is as good as it's going to get. Or they may start searching for meaning in their life and wonder what is their purpose for being here.

Many people will spend years of their life in such a stuck place, and sadly, others will spend their entire lifetime, and yet the biggest reason why they are so stuck is because they simply do not know what they want. This is when you could say that you are literally stuck in a rut, and it can be a major cause of stress. (See book and workshop - It's Your Life, So What Are You Going To Do With It?)

In order to get out of this rut and start moving forward you need to first become crystal clear about what you want, but this is where so many people get stumped. Following are a few tips to help you shake up all of the crud in your mind so that you can start to find some clarity on the subject.

First, start by acknowledging what is not working for you in your life. This is a great place to start because when we are stuck we are typically more aware of what we don't want than of what we do want anyway. But the key here is just to acknowledge and not to get caught up in trying to figure out why we are stuck or how we got ourselves there.

In order to do this you will want to first start by making a list of your negative thoughts and feelings. Write down all of the things in your life that you are not happy with. Put them on a piece paper in the form of a list.

Then when you are done, read through your list and notice how you feel as you read each item on it. Only spend a minute or so thinking about each item on the list, while being very careful not to get caught up in analyzing how, or why this problem came to be. Then, while you have your attention on one individual issue, flip it around by asking yourself the following question: What do I want instead?

Make sure that you do this on an issue by issue basis. I.e. only focus on one item on the list at a time. It doesn't matter at this point whether you think or believe that you can make this change, just answer the question. What do I want instead?

Upon completing your list of wants, go back through your first list, cross out each item and then spend at least a few minutes thinking about the items on your new list. You can now start brainstorming for ideas of how a person could achieve some of these new goals. If you find yourself analyzing, or thinking about all of the reasons why you can't have the more positive choices, just set those thoughts aside, and go back to brainstorming anyway. Do the same for each item.

This is one of the first exercises I do in my goal achievement workshops such as the New Year Resolutions, Goals, Dreams and Aspirations workshop, and It's Your Life – So What Are You Going To Do With It? And people love this exercise.

Be sure to register on my VIP Launch List to receive your invitation to my New Year Resolutions Kickoff Webinar at www.theoneminutestressmanager.com

My workshop It's Your Life, So What Are You Going To Do With was developed precisely for helping people figure out exactly what they want to do with their life.

The Simple Life Does Not Have To Be A Dream

I just heard a great story about a penniless fisherman who was fishing on the beach while his kids played nearby. As he was standing there knee deep in water a well dressed financially successful business man with his gold digger girlfriend, dressed in the latest designer duds approached him. They were enjoying their yearly two week summer vacation.

The wealthy man said to the poor fisherman, hey why do you chose to be a fisherman all your life when you could get a job like mine and earn way more money so that you can save up for a nice retirement on the beach.

The fisherman gazed at the ocean, then looked at the sun setting on the horizon, and finally motioned towards his kids playing in the sand. He then looked straight into the eyes of the stressed out, wealthy business man and said, "But why?"

I love this story.

You Don't Have To Chose Between Love Or Money

It is 2012 and we are living in a time and a place where we in North America have the highest rates of stress, anxiety and depression in the world. We also have more single people than married people for the first time in history and this is not necessarily by choice, and I believe that the isolated lives led by so many of us today is a major contributor to this stress.

I write, speak and teach about dating and relationships and have been very interested in this field for over 20 years, and am very aware of many factors which have contributed to this problem. One of which, according to a lot of men is the fact that women's roles have changed. I truly get how these men think this, however there has been something far more profound going on in North America for many years that has been a bigger contributing factor of this problem.

Besides the fact that women's roles have generally changed, many men have also for reasons of their own, decided to put their own personal lives on hold too. And they too have done so to become better educated, to focus on their careers, and as some would say, to go after the money. Somewhere along the way they too decided to give up the very thing that most men ultimately strive for in life, because somehow they have felt compelled to make a choice. And that choice was to choose between love and money, and unfortunately as a result more and more men are now finding it very difficult to find a wife.

As a result depression rates in men are sky-rocketing and one of the reasons is that many of them cannot find true love, and they feel that the prospects of living out that role of hunter, provider, protector has come under a huge threat. And the sad thing is that so many men have passed up an opportunity of experiencing true love so that they could instead go after the money. Keep in mind, you do not get too many opportunities in life to meet that one special person who could turn out to be your soul mate, so be careful not to miss that opportunity.

Women are also at risk of suffering the same fate, and yet we do have the opportunity to have it all. Don't make the mistake of thinking that you have to choose between love and money, as this seems to be a very North American way of thinking.

Here's the thing. Although I have never met a man who actually set out to be rich, successful, alone and lonely, I have met many who have succeeded at achieving this. And to cap it off, I have spoken to many men who have told me that they would give it all up for love.

Unplug From Distortion And Tune In To Experience Life Through Your Senses

Did you know that when plugged into cell phones, ear phones, or any other sort of electronic device, whether it is via your ears or your eyes you are literally cutting off these senses, or at least to a certain degree. You are no longer fully experiencing your surroundings through your senses, your intuitions are at an all time low, and you are basically dissociated and disconnected. And since so many people who suffer with anxiety experience a similar sense of disconnect and dissociation, I wouldn't think that this could be particularly good for you.

As I mentioned earlier we are mind body entities and we are meant to experience life through our senses. However since so many people complain about feeling disconnected, or that they feel numb in life I thought that I'd throw in a few little tips that might help you tap into your mind body magic.

Here are a couple of little tricks which I teach in my mind body magic class. Try them out to see just how cool this mind body magic really is.

Wake up your brain. This is a really simple exercise that gets your left and right brain communicating with each other. Stand up if you can, although you can do a seated version of this exercise. Raise your left knee as if you were stepping up onto a big step and touch it with your right hand. Then switch legs. Do this in a marching pattern, you can do it from a standing position or while walking.

Here is another little mind body trick. Stand up straight with eyes looking straight ahead. Ask yourself a yes or no question. It could be something as simple as, is my name (state your name here)? Then pay attention to what your body does. See if you notice how you sway. You should feel your body sway backwards or forwards.

Then ask your body to show you a yes response, and pay attention to what it does, can you feel yourself sway backwards or forwards? Take note to see which way you sway for a yes response and then ask your body to show you a no response. See if you can tell the difference.

After you have mastered that you can use this little mind body magic trick to find the answers to anything you may feel some internal conflict over. This is really tapping into your mind body magic as well as into your true awareness.

To become more aware of how you feel, and of what is actually going on in your life, tune into your environment and tap into your mind body magic.

Apologize

What's more difficult, saying you're sorry, or ending a relationship?

Walking around feeling bad about something you may have done wrong, or worse yet knowing that you did something to hurt someone you care about, can be extremely stressful on your body, mind, and soul. But for some people, the thought of saying sorry would be so out of the question, because to them, it would mean that they would either be admitting that they did something wrong, or they may think that they would be admitting to defeat.

Saying sorry has nothing to do with either of these beliefs. Besides, even if it were the case then would it not be worth taking some of the responsibility for the sake of saving a relationship?

If you fear that your apology would not be accepted and that is the reason holding you back, then think about it this way. Your apology will start to lay the foundation of rebuilding that relationship; it will also relieve a great burden from yourself at the same time, and even if the recipient does not show any gratitude for your apology, you will know that deep down inside you have made an effort.

On the other hand, not saying sorry, or making amends would be far more self punishing to yourself than it would to apologize, as to chose to let a relationship go for the price of an apology would be like cutting one's own nose off to spite one's own face.

One last thing, if you are going to apologize for something, make sure that you are genuine, and make it count.

Follow Through On Commitments To Others

Following through on your commitments is a life skill that so many people fail to take seriously, yet the consequences can have a major negative impact on any relationships in your life. This in itself can become a major cause of stress, and here is why.

First of all if you fail to follow through on your commitments to others you are putting those relationships in jeopardy, not to mention that if you let people down on a regular basis you may end up feeling guilty and want to avoid them. Both are negative emotions that cause stress.

Also, if your reason for letting someone down is not genuine, meaning that you have used some lame excuse to get out of a plan, you will know deep down inside, that you are not being completely honest. A lie, no matter how small or insignificant it may seem can actually cause an energy disruption in your body, and when it does you may experience physical, as well as emotional stress.

Then if you consider the fact that every time you let someone down that you are also letting yourself down in the process, meaning that you will probably develop some negative thoughts and feelings about yourself, you will see that this behaviour can become a major source of stress

To eliminate this particular cycle of stress from your life and to avoid earning yourself a bad reputation of being unreliable you can follow these simple tips:

First you can start by being much more careful about what plans you make in the first place. As in don't make any plans with anyone unless you are fully committed to following through on them.

Also don't feel obligated to accept an invitation that you really don't want to accept. It is far more polite to decline an invitation when it is offered, than it is to let someone down after the fact.

Don't kid yourself that you are being nice by agreeing to do something just because you don't want to be honest and decline an invitation. There is actually nothing nice about doing this at all. In fact it is actually really quite rude and inconsiderate to set people up with something to look forward to only to let them down by cancelling later.

Absolutely do not go around making plans with three of four different people so that you can keep your options open while thinking that you can decide who you are going to spend your time with when that time arrives. I know part of the mentality behind this behaviour has come about from living in a time and place where so many people have become so unreliable. The problem is with this behaviour is that you then become part of the problem, and you will then have to let people down too.

Do practice the art of commitment. This may take a little getting used to, especially if you are of the mindset that it is no big deal to cancel on plans. But the truth is that cancelling on plans can, and often does have a very negative impact on everyone involved.

Many people will read this and wonder why I would include such pointer, because they would never personally consider letting anyone down. However, since I now live in a part of the world where the lack of follow through is more the norm, and where this unreliable mentality has become such a huge issue that it is also a major cause of stress in so many people's lives, I decided to add it in.

Since I write, speak and coach about dating and relationships I can tell you that the number one complaint from men and women is the lack of commitment, and the lack of follow through they have experienced when making plans for a date.

I have also been involved with organizing social events, and teaching workshops, and I know a lot of people in the same business, and again, the lack of follow through, and the amount of cancellations is such a huge problem that it creates an enormous amount of stress. And to give you an idea what I'm talking about I've heard that the actual show up rate for most workshops and presentations is typically less than 40%.

I also know a lot of coaches, counsellors and therapists who work in different geographical locations. Each location seems to bring with it its own set of challenges and complaints from clients, but when it comes to this city and working with business owners and managers, one of the biggest sources of stress comes from, you guess it, people not showing up or following through.

When making plans with someone they should be made with the intention of being followed through on. A plan is meant to be a commitment, where as long as both people are genuine, reliable and considerate of other peoples feeling and time, this will more than likely happen.

When we ask someone to do something, or we accept an invitation meaning that we have now made a plan then we are doing two things. First we are tying up each other's time, meaning that we are now not available to accept other invitations, or plan to do something else during that time. And we are giving each other something to look forward too.

If you now cancel or simply do not show up you are literally letting that other person down, at which point they will likely be extremely disappointed, not to mention the fact that they may have in the meantime passed up other opportunities in order to commit to you.

What this means now is not only does it cause stress, guilt and bad feelings on the person who is being unreliable, but it is causing the other person who has been let down to feel disappointed as well. And if this happens on a regular basis, trust, and relationships break down.

This life skill actually one of the most important skills you could develop. After all they say that 80% of success is just showing up, and that applies to anything.

Follow Through On Commitments To Self

Not following through on commitments to others is bad enough, but not following through on commitments to yourself is like giving up on yourself, not to mention your goals, your dreams and your aspirations.

Every time we fail to follow through for ourselves we are feeding the habit of self sabotage, and we are empowering the beliefs that we are not worth our own efforts. We may even start to wonder if we can actually depend on ourselves and whether or not we will always let ourselves down no matter how much we want something.

If we let ourselves down often enough, we may even develop some negative anchors which can sabotage us in any area of our lives. In fact they can be so powerful that they can cause us to give up on our goals or dreams before we even get started, and can prevent us from experiencing any sort of success.

If you are aware that you let yourself down on a regular basis and you are ready to change this habit, then here are a few handy tips.

First, spend a little bit of time thinking about what usually prevents you from following through for yourself to see if you can identify any particular habits, obstacles, fears or objections that seem to get in your way.

Then when you are ready to embark on another plan, or to set out to achieve a new goal or dream, ask yourself why you really want to do it? As you are thinking about these questions pay particular attention to how your responses make you feel. And really pay attention to the feelings which are generated by these thoughts, and not just the thoughts themselves.

Then, when you have decided to commit to a goal, rate it on a scale of 1- 10 for importance and priority. With 1 meaning that it is just a good idea and 10 meaning that you really want to achieve it.

And finally ask yourself the following question. If one year from now, you looked back and realized that you did not follow through, and did not achieve whatever it was that you set out to do, in other words you had let yourself down, how would this make you feel?

There are so many reasons why people let themselves down, and if you really want to change this habit you will need to become crystal clear about what you want, you will need to learn how to identify all of the obstacles, objections, fears and motivational strategies which prevent you from succeeding, and you will need to learn how to set and achieve crystal clear goals.

I teach these skills in my workshop and book called Its Your Life – So What Are You Going To Do With It?

If you don't think that you can make these changes or achieve your goals on your own, then I'd strongly suggest that you hire yourself a coach.

Organize Your Thoughts As Well As Your Life

Disorganization is a major cause of stress not to mention the fact that it can literally sabotage any area of your life. Creating a few new habits can actually turn this around.

First of all even if you don't like to plan ahead, and you'd rather leave everything till last minute, make a promise to yourself to start giving yourself at least a head start. For instance if you are going for a job interview on a Wednesday, get your clothes ready and prepare yourself the night before. That way you won't wake up the morning of your interview to find that the suit you were going to wear is in the laundry hamper and your resume hasn't been updated.

Get into the habit of doing this in every area of your life, and start with your New Year Resolutions. I do this by actually getting started with my New Year Resolutions by spending some time during the week between Christmas and the New Year to decide which New Year Resolutions I am going to make. I then do a bit of preparation so that when January 1st comes along I am all ready to start off the New Year on the right foot.

Create a new habit to start getting one step ahead of yourself as it only takes a few small changes with your organizational skills before you start to reap the rewards. And you will see some very positive results.

Life Is A Balancing Act

Very often when we set out to achieve something in our life we can become so focussed, determined and motivated to go after that one thing that we end up getting tunnel vision, and we can lose sight of what is really most important to us. We may even disconnect from other parts of our life and the results can be devastating.

A good example of this would be when a very career oriented person puts so much time into their education or work that they lose track of people and time. Many men and women fail to realize this until they have spent years of their lives chasing after their goals and material wealth, only to find themselves waking up one day, wondering what they have missed out on. And may even start to question what they are doing it all for.

This happens to those people who make the mistake of becoming so focused on a particular goal that they fall into the trap of ignoring, or even eliminating other aspects of their life. Consequently they end up compartmentalizing their lives so much that they lose sight of whom, or what they value most. And in the process many people even put their lives on hold for so long that lose track of time, and for some it ends up being indefinitely. This could be a very high price to pay for success.

If we ignore our health and wellness, put our love lives on hold, kid ourselves that we do not need a social life, or detach ourselves from community or our spiritual awareness, we run the risk of ending up lonely and alone. And by the time we become aware of our own situation, and realize that the life we have created is not as rewarding as we had hoped it would be, it may be too late or at the least very difficult to get back on track. And this is why we need to make sure that we have balance in our life.

The whole point of having balance is in our life is to remain aware of, and to give attention to all of the parts of our lives that are important to us. This may mean that we need to pay attention to, and to give time to nurturing and developing important relationships, spending time with family and friends, taking care of our health and fitness, being involved in our community, or perhaps volunteering for a special cause. We may also want to practice some sort of spiritual awareness and devote some time to our own personal growth.

Although it may seem difficult to achieve balance we must remember that without it something is probably going to give, and you could end up losing out on some very important aspect of your life. I always use the example that I do not know anyone who set out to be alone, lonely, disconnected, unhealthy, bored and successful, however, I have met many who have unintentionally achieved this. And they have managed to do so because they lost the balance in their lives.

Balance is about being aware of whom you are, what you want, what is important to you, and how you fit into the world around you, and about immersing yourself into each of these areas of your life.

However, for some the idea of having balance in their life may seem to be more of a burden, or even difficult to maintain. As the thought of having to share yourself, or your time amongst your commitments may appear to be more of an obstacle, as it will take away time from something that perhaps you are trying to achieve. If this is a thought that keeps you from maintaining balance in your life then you might want to consider the fact that if you put too many of your interests on hold for the benefit of achieve one thing, you could end up missing out on a lot of what truly matters to you, and possibly even resenting your achievements in the end. With this in mind then we should strive to live a full and balanced life at all times.

If you are ready to start leading a more balanced life but are not sure where to start then here are a few tips. Start by writing a list of all of the areas of your life which are important to you and that you would like to devote more time and energy to.

They may include things such as family, friends, romantic relationships, community, spirituality, personal growth, hobbies, interests, work, play, career, travel, volunteering. You can generate your own ideas and develop your own list.

Then after completing your list think about how much time you would like to devote to each of these areas and how you are going to go about doing it. Starting this process will help you become more aware of what you really want in your life, and having this awareness will inspire you to develop a more balanced and fulfilling life.

Just remember to give each area of your life some attention on a regular basis and to practice devoting some time to maintaining this balance on a daily, weekly and monthly basis.

Become Aware Of Your Thoughts As Well As The Feelings In Your Body

Besides taking stock, and considering what areas of your life may not be working as well as you would like, and coming to terms with some of the things that could be causing you stress, I strongly suggest that you also pay attention to the thoughts and feelings you experience on a daily basis. These could be warning signs, but failing to notice them could allow stress to manifest into much bigger problems which could also end up bringing you down. I know this firsthand from my own experience, so I urge you to pay attention to the signs.

There have been times in my life that I have been so busy, and or so stressed, that I wasn't even aware of what I was feeling in my own body. For instance, I wake up very early in the morning, in the summer I'm well on my way by 6am, and before I even get out of bed I start thinking about what I want to achieve that day. I get up, have my coffee, get ready and start my day and it's not unusual for me to spend a couple of hours doing some work, research, writing or learning something new before I go to work.

Then after putting in a full day I come home, probably workout at the gym, and then spend another 4 – 5 hours working again.

It's also not unusual for me to work 7 days a week, it is September 23rd and I have not taken a single day off since Christmas day. Since I am single I can do this, and I am an extremely productive person. However, the way in which I have been able to maintain this pace for so long has been because without realizing it, there have been times when I've spent much of my life on auto pilot.

What this has meant is that there have been times when I have become so tired that I became burnt out because I missed the warning signs. For instance, when I was hairdressing I never used to eat breakfast or lunch and pretty much lived on black coffee all day. I always had a ton of energy but somehow never felt the pain in my feet or back until I would sit down at the end of the day after standing in high heel shoes for hours. Nor did realize that the reason I always felt cold was because of poor circulation which had been brought on by standing for too long, not eating properly, and drinking way too much coffee.

Then for the longest time I lived an extremely busy and chaotic life until one day I suddenly came over feeling really quite ill. In fact it started happening on a regular basis but I couldn't figure out what was wrong with me. This had been going on for quite some time before one night I actually stopped to think about it, and it was only then, at about midnight when realized that I had not stopped since 6am and had been on the go for about 18 hours. And although that was how I was spending most of my days I had failed to recognize how tired and exhausted I was until I started to feel ill.

These are the types of warning signs that we need to be paying attention too. I know this must sound crazy but the truth is so many people live their lives in the same disconnected, chaotic way that I did. And they too experience similar feelings or symptoms in their bodies which they do not clue in to until it is too late. This lack of awareness can cause anyone to become a burnout victim, waiting to happen.

The same can be said for emotions. I know a lot of people who suffer with all sorts of strange symptoms in their bodies which cause them to feel ill. They may get headaches, backaches or a stomach upset, or they may simply feel out of sorts, but they cannot figure out what is wrong with them. But what they fail to recognize is that because they are putting their attention on a lot of negative things, and focus on all of the bad things in life, it is likely the thoughts in their minds that are causing their symptoms. But again, most people don't even realize what thoughts are going through their heads never mind how those thoughts are affecting them on a physical level.

Whenever you start to experience feelings or sensations in your body, then the best thing to do is stop, and check in with yourself. Ask your unconscious mind why are you feeling this way, and what is causing these feelings. And then take a moment to think about what is on your mind and remember that since we are mind body entities, and our thoughts initiate corresponding feelings that we need to be careful of what we put our attention on.

Knowing the answers to these questions will allow you to take the appropriate actions and relieve your symptoms and put your body back into balance. Having a keen awareness of what is going on in your mind as well as your body will be a major key to allowing you to achieve the types of experiences that you would like in your life.

Live Your Life On Purpose In Order To Nourish Your Body Mind And Soul

Every time we eat, drink, taste, breath, think, see, hear, touch, feel, sense, or smell something, we are taking in life via all of our senses, and by doing so we are literally feeding our body, mind and soul. Some of what we take in will help to nourish, sustain, and even empower us to the point that we could live our lives to the fullest. But then other things may be detrimental to everything we do. Knowing this we should decide right here and now to become very aware of what we chose to accept into our lives.

Think about this for a moment. If you started to eat something that tasted absolutely disgusting, would you continue to eat it or would you spit it out with disgust? What about if you turned on your radio to hear the most annoying music that was just grinding on your nerves, would you turn it up hoping that you would get used to it or would you change the station to find something much more uplifting? And if you noticed a noxious smell that was bad enough to turn your stomach, would you remove yourself to get away from it, or would you hope that it would eventually subside? And if you turned on your television to see something really disturbing would you force yourself to watch it, or would you find something much easier on the mind. And finally if you did something that caused you a great deal of physical pain would you continue to do it anyway or would you avoid it like the plague? And if something scared you so bad that it frightened the living daylights out of you, would you stay in harm's way or would you retreat to safety?

Most functioning human beings, and animals for that matter would more often than not remove themselves from any situation that caused them distress or discomfort. So why then do we not do the same when something is hurting our mental, emotional or spiritual wellbeing?

The answer may have to do with awareness, as in, we may not become motivated enough to make changes in our own lives until we have reached a point of real discomfort. And the danger in this could be that if we don't reach that turning point, we may simply ignore the warning signs, or learn to tolerate our discomfort and never find the motivation to change.

The sad thing is that many of us will never experience that level or intensity of discomfort that will cause us to wake up, take action and seek change. This would mean that in the end, it could be the more subtle problems in your life which could ultimately cause you more pain.

If any of this is ringing a bell for you, then I suggest that you make a conscious decision to wake up and become more aware of, and tune in to what is really going on in your life, *and* in the world around you. Make the decision right now to start paying more attention to what is, or is not working in your life, and set some new guidelines and boundaries as to what you will or will not tolerate.

Commit to becoming the best version of yourself possible and living the life you were meant to live. And tap into your creativity to figure out how you can achieve a life full meaning, and start living your life with passion and on purpose.

You do have the power to choose how you live and how you will experience life. All you have to do is wake up, and I mean that in every sense of the word. You need to start living your life more consciously and to become very aware of who or what is helping or hurting you.

You do not have to go through life living as a victim of circumstance. In fact you can chose right now to live your life on purpose, because ultimately it is your life so you should be the one who chooses what you do with it.

Live your life with passion and on purpose.

With peace, love and harmony

Suzanne

Suzanne@suzanneprice.com

NOTES

NOTES

NOTES

NOTES

Other Books & Programs Written By Suzanne J. Price

It's Your Life – So What Are You Going To Do With It?

New Year Resolutions, Goals, Dreams & Aspirations

How To Turn That First Glance Into A Date.

Tapping Into Your Mind Body Connection

To learn about upcoming live and online workshops as well as book launches, please add your name to my VIP Launch List at www.theoneminutestressmanager.com

Also visit

www.thesinglestimes.com

www.peoplepoweredcoaching.com

www.suzanneprice.com